Rosie Rabbit has a radish.

Rosie takes good care of her radish.
She rakes the ground around it.
She removes rocks.

Rosie rakes and rakes—even in the rain!
She does not rest.

"Come for a ride," says Rick Rooster.
"Let's roller-skate," says Rita Raccoon.

But Rosie would rather take care
of her radish.

At night, Rosie sits in her rocking chair.
She reads to her radish and plays the radio.

The radish grows and grows.
Soon the radish is ripe.
It is ready to be picked.

Rosie ties a rope around the radish.
Rick and Rita help her pull up the radish root.

What a rare radish!
It is red and round and really big!

Rick and Rita help Rosie roll the radish
down the road.

What will Rosie do with her radish?

She will take it to the fair…

and win a blue ribbon!

How many things can you find that begin with the letter R?

See inside back cover for answers.

Rr Cheer

R is for rabbit, radish, and rose

R is for ribbon and the rooster that crows

R is for run, rope, rock, and red

R is for raindrops that fall on your head

Hooray for **R**, big and small—

the most remarkable letter of all!